Small Observations

Kay Hefferan

Small Observations

Acknowledgements

Some of these poems have been published previously:
'Robyn Gordon': Poetry 2000 at Willunga 1995
'Standing on the footbridge': Multi Links (Noarlunga) 1995
'Berwick Street 1944': Multi Links (Noarlunga) 1995
'Early autumn apple': *Friendly Street Reader* 1996
'Wattle where?': First Prize Poetry Unplugged 2001

My thanks and appreciation to Margaret Bolton from North Eastern Writers Inc. for her assistance with editing, support and encouragement. Also to Lynda Pooley from Books in Clover for reading, support and encouragement.

For my grandchildren, Alexandra and Griffin

Small Observations
ISBN 978 1 76041 572 3
Copyright © Kay Hefferan 2018

First published 2018 by
GINNINDERRA PRESS
PO Box 3461 Port Adelaide 5015
www.ginninderrapress.com.au

Contents

Nature	7
After Choir	9
Lizards	10
Charlotte	11
Wanderer Butterfly	12
Hens	13
Early Autumn Apple	14
Rainforest	15
Diamond Duck	16
Blackbird	17
Robyn Gordon	18
Parrots and Pears	19
Daily Routine	20
Swallows in Spring	21
Holidays	23
Walk by the Livingstone	25
Standing on the Footbridge	26
Berwick Street, 1944	27
Wattle Where?	28
High Country	29
Oriental Claims	30
The Flock	31
The Trip Home	32
Kakadu	35
Miscellaneous	37
Wood 'n' Ice Man	39
One Dark Night	41
The New Mum	42
The Knee Rug	43

Joy	44
Happiness	45
Candle Gazing	46
Candlelight	47
Adelaide Arcade	48
Hundreds and Thousands	49
Mademoiselle	50
The Shoe Sales Lady	51
Toy Cat	52
The Gas Box	53
Christmas Tree	54
Story Cubes	55
My Dad	56
Three Trees	57
Turtle Dove	58
Twinkle Toes	59
Noarlunga Holidays	60

Nature

After Choir

Down at the beach
lots of smooth round stones
dotted the sand
little waves
kept splashing
planes flew low
over our heads.
At home we ate
mango and blueberries
before you painted
yellow chickens.

Lizards

Lizards darting here and there
warm rocks coax them out
shiny black with rainbow tinge
they lie there soaking up sun.
See them dart when
the dog wanders by
or a bird flies near
back into the creepers
they wriggle
until the coast is clear.

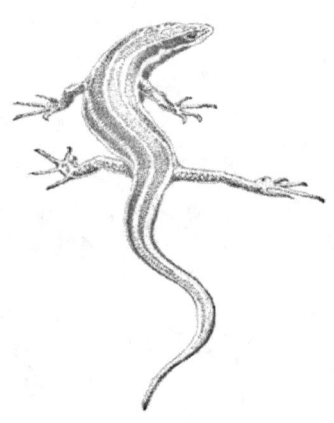

Charlotte

In the early morning sun
silken strands of fine gold
catch the light
long gossamer threads
anchor a golden veil
as it hangs between
mandarins and oranges
each night she waits
for the unsuspecting
to fall into the trap.
Bundled in silk they
wait to join the line
of empty shells
the contents already
consumed.

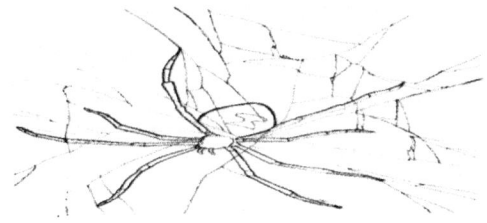

Wanderer Butterfly

The green capsule
hangs by a thread
tossed by the wind
warmed by the sun
fed from within
it grows
ready for birth
pushing, stretching
the capsule bursts
crumpled wings
slow to unfold
black framework
stretched to its tips
burnished orange
flashes brilliant
quivers then rests
a final flutter
she soars into life

Hens

Chook chook chook
they come running
their favourite treat
has just arrived
greens
lettuce, silver beet
thistles, kale and cabbage
frenzied pecking and
an occasional
squabble over one leaf.

As they ingest these
culinary delights
I ponder the
transfiguration
of greens
the circular motion
the connection of all things
and the eggs that will
be collected tomorrow.

Early Autumn Apple

Teeth pierce rosy skin
it snaps
is torn away.
Open cut soothed
by rising juice
sparkling in the sunlight.
Cheeks wince
teeth squeak as
crisp flesh polishes
them clean.
Each bite reduces
until it reaches
the core.
A titbit for the sparrows.

Rainforest

From daylight
to inner darkness
where shafts of light
slice the trees and
spotlight exotic
toadstools standing to
attention
red helmets cocked
and spotted.
Whipbirds report our
presence as they crack.
Giant blue wings flutter
indecisively
vines tangle and hinder
as we pass
treading the soft leafy carpet
inches thick, woven gently
leaf upon bark under twig.
This forest
a time capsule carrying
the past into the future.

Diamond Duck

Diamond lives in
a private zoo
sharing a pen with
a kangaroo.

Diamond
is a beautiful bird
black and tan feathers
and a white neckband.

Diamond has
a temper so bad
he chases the keeper
quacking too loud
flapping his wings
entertaining the crowd

Diamond duck and his
irritable mood
keeps the keeper running
when he comes with food.
Nobody knows why
Diamond's temper is
so bad, just
beware when you visit
don't enter his yard.

Blackbird

A few short steps across the lawn
she cocks her eye toward the grass
statue still as seconds pass
before the fatal stab.

Poor worm.

He disappears in sections
into the golden beak
she lifts her head in triumph
and satisfied
she sings.

Robyn Gordon

Pink hand reaches out
long tendril fingers
beckon
honeyeaters answer
her call.

Family groups gather
crowds titter as
trapeze birds swing on
reddish blooms.

Garden tap gushes
birds vanish
no time to bid
farewell.

Parrots and Pears

Raucous cackling
shatters morning quiet
rainbow lorikeets
sharing breakfast
in the pear tree.
Fruit juice drips
from their beaks
nibbled pears reveal
sparkling white flesh.
Below, the ground is littered with
pear droppings and cores
morning sun highlights
vivid red, blue and
green feathers
peeking through leaves.
Birds' breakfasts so absorbing
they don't notice me.

Daily Routine

Late afternoon
autumn gold lingers
the New Holland
gang arrives
it's bath time.
A dozen pairs of
wings flap and splash
birds dart in and out
of the water
stopping to shake
and preen on nearby
branches.
Minutes of
high-pitched chatter
then…
they scream away
a squadron
on a mission.

Swallows in Spring

Gliding and swooping
blue-black feathers and
long forked tails
two busy birds
fly back and forth
a mud crafted nest
grows under the eaves
before four dots of fluff
with bright yellow beaks
sit on the rim.
Two busy parents
fly back and forth
snap up insects on the wing
a task they share to
feed the chicks.
Fluff turns to feathers
beaks grow strong
six birds now
gliding, swooping
flying back and forth

Holidays

Walk by the Livingstone

Pooh sticks ride the rapids
on the Livingstone
downstream they rush
past naked willows
over pebbles and clumps
of other Pooh sticks
snagged on tree roots.

On the banks
under cover of
dry gum leaves
and pine needles
the dark eyes of old
banksia men stare.

A wallaby thumps nearby
brown fur winter thick
shines rich in the sun
once out of reach
he perches on a rock
and checks out the intruders.

Standing on the Footbridge

over the Onkaparinga

A lifetime ago I was here
then it was far from the city
a half-day trip by bus
holidays between sea and rolling farm.

I remember the river
running deep and clear
today an ageing reptile
it snakes through sand and swamp
sick from the weight of suburbia
searching for renewal.

Cliffs still stand
like half-eaten gateau
cut by the river's flow
white sand tongue
licks toward the mouth
holding back the sea.

Hope clings in pleas
from circling gulls
seagrass growing behind fences
and the smiles of walkers
passing on the footbridge.

Berwick Street, 1944

A tiny cottage
on a windblown block
between a farm and a fortress
white slurried walls
dark timber battens
a game board on the ceiling.
Shadows danced each night
before an oil lantern
wood crackled in the stove
cooking and warming
heavy curtains hung
drawn on wooden rings.
Outside pink tassels
hung from tamarisk trees
wild flowers
dotted bending grass
as it whispered in the wind.
Limestone rock mottled
a caramel road
that led to forever
sand hills, pure and simple
held back the sea
to release the river.

Mullet caught with cockles
in the early hours
Whiting in the evening
on the bend
sleep came in iron beds
to the rhythm of waves
rumbling on the beach.

Wattle Where?

Railway yards
cold hard steel
stacked rails
and fencing
except for
one wattle sapling.
Golden yellow puffs
a slender trunk
bending slightly
stretching up
through heavy-gauge rubble
parallel lines
and galvanised sheds
together
reflecting silver and gold
in the morning sun.

High Country

Long shadows stretch
across the valley.
tan and white cattle graze.
Answering the shrill
of the stockman's whistle
dogs muster bleating sheep
into a whirlpool of wool.

A nearby stream bends
and babbles
through bronze-tipped willows.
Evening sky and hills
merge blue-grey
in the distance
as stockmen and dogs
drive the woolly mob home.

Oriental Claims

Time worn and faded
water-hewn walls
shaped by hungry men
in pursuit of riches promised.

Silent organ pipes
carved cathedral spires
stand deserted
scarred and overgrown.

Nearby pines whisper
tales of men from
distant lands
their hands calloused
backs bent and broken.

In their quest for gold
in a land far from home
they have carved
this monument into
the history of our land.

The Flock

Winter twilight
a mountain backdrop
dark and silent
keeper of secrets.
A billowing white sail
flows back and forth
against the forest

falling
        rising
falling

screeching
squabbling
the flock settles
as night falls
over Omeo.

The Trip Home

It was 9.30 p.m.
the train rolled from the platform
the first autumn rain
striped the window
millions of lights
glittered over the
suburbs
wet roads glossy black
reflected red crossing lights
as the train gathered speed.

A night spent
in a roomette
and carried overland
during sleep.
Soft dawn light
gave birth to a new day.
In the window
moving pictures of
farmers tending cows
feeding chooks and ploughing fields.
In a backyard
a rusty boat high on stilts
stands unfinished
threaded with weeds
a dream not yet fulfilled
or a dream in ruins.

A bridge spans the River Murray
chequered green flats
at the river's edge
dotted with cows.
Passing through
Murray Bridge
memories of busy
riverboats with bales
piled high
play in my mind.
Through the window
more cows, chestnut horses
and sheep.

Train speed begins to slow
bending and winding
the steep gradient
suggests the approach
into Adelaide.
Through the window
people prepare for
the day ahead
picking up the paper
putting out bins
leaving for work.

A taxi takes me
from the station.
At home
I pick up the paper
put out the bins
and begin my day
with memories of
shopping till I dropped
and sharing it
with a friend.

Kakadu

Floating
on a flat-bottomed boat
inches from the water
hundreds
of whistling ducks
herd
along the banks
yet there is quiet.
In the distance magpie geese
fly in great profusion
ahead a crocodile
crosses our watery path
floating eyes protruding.
A jabiru pecks
in the mud,
pacing over lily pads
a Jesus bird is
sacrificed to a croc
with barely a sound.

Miscellaneous

Wood 'n' Ice Man

A stout maroon jumper
sits under a well-worn hat
legs dangle over the dray
as the horse trots his
slow even pace.
Pneumatic tyres
whisper to the tar.

He visits early
in summer
before the ice melts.
At each stop
behind the cart
Kevin shapes
and chisels each block.
With grappling hook and
leather glove
he lifts the frozen load
a trail of wet dots follow
as he lumbers to the house.
'Ice,' he calls and doors fly open
kitchen floors suffer as
ice crashes into the chest.
Chips splatter, lid slams down
'Seeya Friday, Ma'am' he shouts
and blunders on his way.

In winter
he brings wood and coal.
The dark green cart
stacked high with logs
and neat bags of coal
the loads are dropped
in small backyards
from lanes at the rear.
For over forty years
he delivered
to customers far and wide
but Saturdays were for
following sport and
Sundays were for church.
Missed by friends and customers
he leaves fond memories
of a time gone by.

One Dark Night

Like lead, shot
from a cannon
the FJ spat
across the road
into the factory fence
a safety net
between injured pride
and horror.

Green and dented
it backed off
the bumper scraped
the road
with a rev or two
it sped away.
No one to ever know
how the fence was wrecked.

Except me.

The New Mum

Much is new
for a first-time Mum
feeding, bathing,
washing nappies
soothing a crying child
fresh air is all important
specially if it's fine
put the pram in the garden
hang nappies on the line
baby sleeping in the pram
everything is fine.
Except – the weather
a shower of rain
brings Mother outside
to bring the washing in.
While folding nappies on the bench
she remembered…

baby is still outside!

The Knee Rug

Thousands of stitches
holding each other tight
row after row their
separate colours glow
with the pride
of their creator
busy fingers
winter evenings
spent
hooking woollen threads
one into the other
and watching them grow
into a gift of love
shyly given
to warm elderly knees.

Joy

At one hour
a soft pink bundle
against my cheek.
Golden hue for hair
five tiny fingers
grip one.

At one year
head down crawling fast
serious business.
Books to read again
and again
hair
still a golden hue.

At two years
running everywhere
what's this?
What's that?
See the tram, ding, dong.
Hair
golden curls bobbing.
I luv you Nan
says my granddaughter.

Happiness

Big brown eyes
and a twinkling smile
convey his sense of
humour.
He loves to laugh
and have others laugh too
and share his big firm hugs.
Collecting eggs
is a lot of fun
and watching Frisbees
flying high or low.
Cricket not so easy
the bat a bit too tall
for a boy just four

but then,
he can chase the ball.

Candle Gazing

The golden flame
flickers briefly
steadies
stretches
its needle point
piercing the darkness
thin smoke
strings into space
curls
as hot wax
dribbles
sculpting stalactites
over the sides
of the candle.

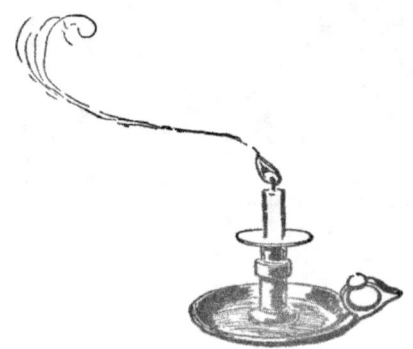

Candlelight

A single flute
the only sound
a single flame
the only light.

Together
they stretch
and waver
each to their peak
creating a space
in which
to dream.

Adelaide Arcade

Crowds pushed
against barriers
necks strained to see
dignitaries stepped
back in time
on inlaid tiles
potted palms dotted
terracotta and marble
Federation green
fringed the mezzanine
coffee aroma
wafted near
wrought-iron tables
shop doorways opened
inviting shoppers in
and light poured
through glass from above.

Hundreds and Thousands

Ladies in large hats
slowly descending
the escalator.
Puffed-up dresses
made of sponge rubber
in shades of pink and blue
eyes hidden by the
broad brims of their hats.
A giant plastic box
of nonpareils
was thrown from above.
People stared as they burst
all over the shop floor
a deep pool of tiny
coloured balls.
The ladies stepped
demurely into the sea
of rainbow colours…

And then, I woke up.

Mademoiselle

Softly she mews
as if to say
'Hello, glad you're back
I know you've been away.'
Her jet fur shining
in the afternoon sun
white bib and whiskers
all washed – and done.
A tiny head cocked
as if to ask
'Just a morsel
when you've finished your tasks.'
He always said
he hated cats
they ruin the garden
and pee on the mats
but this little lady
brought down his defences.
All cuddles and croons
he's quite out of his senses.

The Shoe Sales Lady

Covered with a trench coat
imagine her surprise
when taking off the coat at work
she found no skirt inside
just a lacy petticoat
jet black as was required.

She joined with the peals of
laughter
and blamed the kids and the rain
a trip to another department
was all that did remain?
Another skirt was needed
before she could work again.

Toy Cat

The old black cat
is no longer there
watching over me
he used to sit on
the mantelpiece
his green eyes staring.

One day
my mother
gave him away
to a child
younger than me.
'You're a big girl now,'
she said.
'You don't need
baby toys.'

The guilt I felt
made me agree
though I didn't
want him to go
'cause he'd always
been there above
my bed and now
I miss him so.

The Gas Box

The gas box
was made of wood
a metre high and
attached to the fence.
Its flat top
a perfect spot to sit
to watch the world go by
workers from railway yards
others came from ETSA
pushing their bikes
against the wind
a day's work left behind
neighbours home from shopping
others pushing prams.
I sat for hours
watching until
it was time for tea.

Christmas Tree

Silver garlands
on velvet branches
a million strands
of shimmering tinsel
and dangling baubles
mirror one another.
Tiny trumpets
herald the coming season
as small Santas
dart between pine needles.
Beneath the spreading branches
mysteries wrapped in red and green
boxes large and small must wait
until the time is right
when the room will burst into Christmas
and masses of coloured paper and ribbon
scatter
revealing
the secrets
that taunted
children's excitement
unleashed at last.

Story Cubes

Nine dice-like cubes
incongruous images
on every side
>a walking stick
>a fish
>a comedy mask
>a bridge

items with no connection.
A story may tell
of a man with a walking stick
who catches a fish
from the bridge
while an onlooker laughs
the moon may be shining
a wand may be waving
the footprint and the arrow
spark some thoughts
a challenge to create
stories that connect
from nine images
in each throw.

My Dad

My dad made things
all kinds of things
he was a fitter and turner
but he made things like ice blocks
on a frosty night
green milky ones.
He made me a musical
triangle
and a dolls house
he bred canaries
he built an aviary
Dad grew the best tomatoes
and beautiful petunias
bright pink swathes of them
the lawn always green
and free of weeds.
When I married he
made me an iron pot stand
and a letter box
marked twenty-two.
For grandchildren there
was an elephant rocker
a blackboard and easel.
Dad liked to read a lot
we talked and
rode our bikes to
collect cow manure
in the parklands.

Three Trees

Three dead trees
the result of neglect
and seasons of drought
standing side by side
on the corner
gnarled and knotted
naked arms outstretched
a sad and lonely plea
to be removed.

A week later
as if answering
the plea
the trees were gone.

Turtle Dove

There he sat
on the sill
inside my window
still as he could be
a regal looking bird
soft grey plumage tinged
with pink
his necked wrapped
in a dotted band
he entered via the chimney
a surprise for he and me
he fell like Alice
into a black hole
and found an unknown land.
I moved toward him slowly
sweet talking as I went
closed my hands around him
and carried him outside
his chance for freedom
postponed a while for
he sat quietly on my palm
perhaps to say thank you
before he flew away.

Twinkle Toes

Shoes have changed
they used to be brown
leather with lace-ups
some black with buckles.
I once had a pair
with snakeskin toes.

Now the colours
are many:
navy with pea green
or purple with pink
made of woven stuff
with thick rubber soles.

The pair I'm buying
have green flashing lights
as long as you jump
and move about.
Grandson is as happy
as I was
with snakeskin toes.

Noarlunga Holidays

Sunny holidays
by the jetty
on a rug.
Sandcastles
and swings
midday treats
shiny pies
from Cuttings.
The hurdy-gurdy
fun to ride
but not after
strawberry milk.

Long walks home
through the swamp.
Dad up front
like Moses.
'Watch out for
Joe Blake,' he'd cry
and we did
as we wound
single file
through sand-mud
and saltbush.

www.ingramcontent.com/pod-product-compliance
Lightning Source LLC
Chambersburg PA
CBHW062202100526
44589CB00014B/1914